1,001 People That Suck

by Kerri Kochanski

1,001 PEOPLE THAT SUCK

Copyright © 2013 by Kerri Kochanski

www.1001peoplethatsuck.com

All rights reserved. No portion of this publication may be reproduced, stored in a retrieval system, or transmitted by any means – electronic, mechanical, photocopying, recording, or any other – except for brief quotations printed in reviews, without the prior written permission of the author.

Kickie Publishing, Second Printing, USA.
ISBN-13: 978-1482319408
ISBN-10: 1482319403

For more information, please contact the author at:
kerrikochanski@gmail.com

	INTRODUCTION	i
1	**1,001 PEOPLE THAT SUCK**	
	The Heartless…………………………………	25
	Selfish & Greedy…………………………..	33
	Pretentious, Glossy & Slick………………….	47
	Scary……………………...……………….	57
	Mysterious & Covert……………………..	63
	Model Citizens?……………………………..	75
2	**OUT & ABOUT**	89
	Road………………………...…………….	91
	Beach……………………………………..	97
	Gym………………………………………..	105
	Shopping………………………………….	111
	College……………………………………	123

3	**IN THE NEIGHBORHOOD**	135
	Domestically Speaking.............................	143
	In Social Situations.................................	149
	Holidays & Occasions..............................	157
4	**PERSONALLY SPEAKING**	169
	Food, Hygiene & Manners.........................	179
5	**IN SCHOOL & AROUND THE WORLD**	191
6	**DISAPPOINTMENTS**	203
7	**UNDER BRIDGES & IN CREVICES**	215
	Mean...	227
	Vain & Vicious..	243
8	**THE WORST**	253
	Vindictive..	267
	Vile...	277
9	**HEARTBREAKERS**	287
	MORE PEOPLE…	295
	ACKNOWLEDGMENTS	318

INTRODUCTION

By 2050, the world's population is expected to increase by 30%. Unfortunately, while the population continues to grow, so do the amount of people who continue to exhibit "bad humanity."

What can you do?

Surely you can't threaten these people with violence. For violence would only lead to an arrest, and an unpleasant stay in jail (for you).

Instead, you can commiserate through this book, and on the blog:

www.1001peoplethatsuck.com

~

And you can take some satisfaction in knowing that said people have been officially classified as:

People That Suck

Enough is enough.

1,001 PEOPLE THAT SUCK

∞

People that burn the American flag.

∞

People that burn the American flag, because they can.

∞

People that elope, and deny their family a wedding.

∞

People that spend too much money on weddings.

∞

People that don't change the toilet paper,
when it's down to the last sheet.

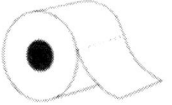

∞

People that bitch.

∞

People that bore.

∞

People that **do not** hold the door.

∞

People that tattle.

∞

People that squeal.

∞

People that cannot keep it **real**…

∞

People that lock you in the closet.

∞

People that flatten your soufflé.

∞

People that climb on drowning swimmers.

∞

People that darken someone's day.

People that smudge a person's window.

∞

People that dent another's door.

∞

People that shirk responsibility.

∞

People that **fuel** other people's wars.

∞

People that can't keep someone's secret.

∞

People that won't give you a break.

∞

People that don't say "please" or "thank you."

∞

People that criticize your weight.

∞

People that think they're "so important."

∞

People that **misspell** other's names.

∞

People that blab about their ailments.

∞

People that **hide**, from where they came.

∞

People that sleep with people's spouses.

∞

People that piss on your parade.

∞

People that tear down someone's castle.

∞

People that **shun** lesbians and gays.

∞

People that park in people's driveways.

∞

People that peek into your drawer.

∞

People that peer in people's windows.

∞

People that scuff up other's floors.

∞

People that **leave you**, for the nanny.

∞

People that throw you to the dogs.

∞

People that kidnap people's children.

∞

People that sue, without good cause.

∞

People that litter on the highway.

∞

People that clog up people's bowls.

∞

People that leave pee on the toilet.

∞

People that tell you where to go.

∞

People that tell you, you're a

∞

People that make you play the fool.

∞

People that get you into trouble.

∞

People that pee in someone's pool.

∞

People that stomp through people's gardens.

∞

People that flit through people's lives.

∞

People that **do not** count their blessings.

∞

People that **don't** apologize.

"Would it kill you?"

∞

People that make up "lame" excuses.

∞

People that do not do their part.

∞

People that don't leave tips for wait staff.

∞

People that cut out Music/Art.

∞

People that **always** ask for favors.

∞

People that moan and groan and whine.

∞

People that tell you you "look tired."

∞

People that leave their friends behind.

∞

People that don't have any loyalty.

∞

People that don't show any class.

People that promote a "false intelligence."

∞

People that grab a person's ass.

∞

People that read through people's emails.

People that spread another's dirt.

∞

People that snipe people on **eBay**.

∞

People that say mean things that hurt.

People that claim that they are "Jesus."

People that renege on a dare.

∞

People that spill the beans on Santa.

People that meddle in your affairs.

∞

People that think their shit don't smell bad.

People that claim they're always **right**.

∞

People that don't re-use/recycle.

∞

People that like to start a fight.

People that bring babies to bar rooms.

∞

People that wish you weren't born.

∞

People that **don't** return the favor.

∞

People that try to outlaw porn.*

∞

People that make a person feel bad.

∞

People that let another fail.

∞

People that think they are "entitled."

∞

People that don't return lost mail.

 *I like porn.*

~

People that make a person worry.

∞

People that make a person wait.

∞

People that **do not** keep their promise.

∞

People that like to AGGRAVATE.

THE HEARTLESS

THE HEARTLESS

∞

People that **never even** have a minute.

∞

People that **never ever** get a clue.

∞

People that do not understand it.

∞

People that place the blame on **you**.

∞

People that say they **do not** love you.

∞

People that claim they **just don't** care.

∞

People that act like they are "better."

∞

People that *never knew* you were there.

THE HEARTLESS

People that cut you, when you're bleeding.

People that blind you, when they drive.

∞

People that stand by, and do **nothing**.

∞

People that skin a seal alive.*

People that ruin people's chances.

∞

People that love another less.

∞

People that will not let you help them.

People that won't give it a **rest**.

 *Really?!*

People that get on people's cases.

∞

People that grate on someone's nerves.

∞

People that don't return your invite.

∞

People that twist up people's words.

∞

People that holler at your children.

∞

People that rile up your pet.

∞

People that launch a cyber-virus.

∞

People that re-gift what they get.

THE HEARTLESS

People that push other people's buttons.

People that pull a person's leg.

∞

People that do not take the "high road."

∞

People that make another beg.

∞

People that engage in "ho̵n̵or killings."
                              ^

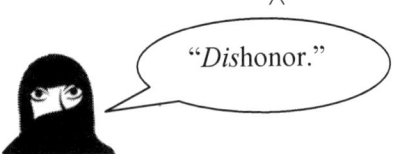
"*Dishonor.*"

People that **do not** value life.

People that drive cars, when they're drinking.

∞

People that take a second wife.

"There's enough on this planet for everyone's **needs**, but not for everyone's **greed**."*

*Mahatma Gandhi (1869-1948)

SELFISH & GREEDY

∞

People that don't protect their children.

∞

People that don't think for themselves.

∞

People that run you through the paces.

∞

People that put others through hell.

∞

People that don't work for a living.

∞

People that call you up to vent.

∞

People that **take**, but aren't **giving**.

1,001 PEOPLE THAT SUCK

∞

People that are in the **1%**.*

*Lucky bastards.*

∞

People that do not pay their taxes.

∞

People that will not yield the floor.

∞

People that spin off onto tangents.

∞

People that leave you wanting more.

∞

People that often act **impossible**.

People that are always **just plain** rude.

∞

People that can't complete instructions.

People that do not follow through.

∞

People that take, because they're **greedy**.

∞

People that go, so they'll be "seen."

∞

People that stay, because they're "needy."

∞

People that cause an ugly scene.

∞

People that fake a serious illness.

∞

People that pull a deadly prank.

∞

People that tend to overthink it.

∞

People that make economies **tank**.

People that steal a person's aura.

People that block somebody's chi.

∞

People that fail to rise above it.

∞

People that **will not** let it be.

∞

People that tip a person's balance.

People that cash another's check.

People that taint somebody's credit.

People that don't pay off their debts.

SELFISH & GREEDY

∞

People that preach Propitiation.*

∞

People that kill, in the name of "God."

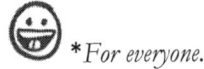 *For everyone.*

People that can't hold conversations.

∞

People that act like complete **snobs**.

∞

People that buy a person's silence.

∞

People that bust another's balls.

∞

People that sell a person's baby.

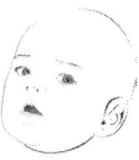

∞

People that **don't support** your cause.

SELFISH & GREEDY

People that **cap** a person's salary.

∞

People that block you from their **tweets**.

∞

People that look over your shoulder.

∞

People that drive from the backseat.*

∞

People that crunch a person's timeline.

People that welch on someone's bet.

∞

People that gamble people's money.

 *Shut up.*

∞

People that make you get upset.

*Bernard Baily (1916-1996)

PRETENTIOUS, GLOSSY & SLICK

PRETENTIOUS, GLOSSY & SLICK

People that ask too many questions.

People that tell too many tales.

∞

People that put on too much perfume.

People that scratch you with their nails.*

∞

People that leave their prints on photos.

People that put their paws on pets.

∞

People that fuck up someone's mojo.

Ouch.

∞

People that saddle you with debt.

∞

People famous for being "famous."

∞

People guilty of being cruel.

∞

∞

People that do things that are shameless.

∞

People that act like a real **tool**.

∞

People that serve up people's pink slips.

∞

People that spike a person's drink.

∞

People that drool on people's shoulders.

∞

People that drape themselves in mink.

PRETENTIOUS, GLOSSY & SLICK

∞

People that notice people's knockoffs.

∞

People that like to goad and taunt.

∞

People that let a person suffer.

People that **waste**, what others **want**.

∞

People that have what "others" are having.

People that fear what "they" might say.

∞

People that don't stand up for justice.

People that look the other way.

People that blind you with their diamonds.

People that slap you in the face.

∞

People that **STOP**, and look you over.

People that don't gain any weight.

People that aren't **open-minded**.

∞

People that will not let you be.

∞

People that don't see the "big picture."

People that ***prize*** celebrity.

*Jonathan Swift (1667-1745)

SCARY

SCARY

People that do not pay it forward.

People that **will not** make it right.

∞

People that sexually harass you.

∞

People that stalk you in the night.

∞

People that strike you as a "user."

∞

People that don't own their mistakes.

∞

People that prove they are **sore losers**.

∞

People that let it escalate.

People that track a person's movements.

∞

People that make a person leave.

∞

People that try hard to "control" you.

∞

People that will not let you breathe.

∞

People that hold a person **hostage**.

∞

People that wreck another's deal.

∞

People that assume they are "exceptions."

SCARY

∞

People that **kill**, so they can *feel*.

People that drive their cars, with vengeance.

People that make a "left" on red.

People that do not stop at stop signs.

∞

People that say what you just said.

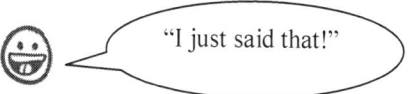

People that look, but do not see you.

People that pray, but don't "believe."

People that try (and want) to be you.

∞

People that have tricks up their sleeve.

MYSTERIOUS & COVERT

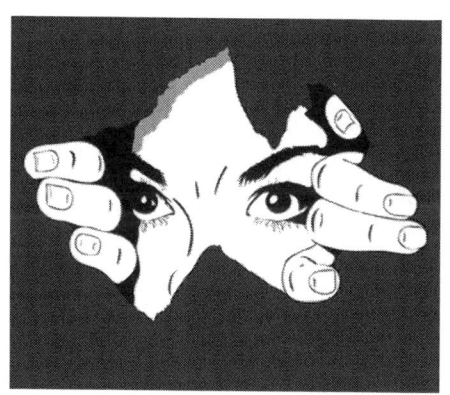

MYSTERIOUS & COVERT

People that use you as a "cover."

People that keep you in the dark.

∞

People that make their mistress "public."

∞

People that deface museum art.

People that blackmail politicians.

∞

People that bust on someone's friends.

∞

People that hit their wives and girlfriends.

∞

People that **borrow**, but don't **lend**.

∞

People that enable an **addiction**.

∞

People that fuel a person's fear.

∞

People that have gigantic egos.

∞

People that yell in people's ears.

∞

People that curse another's spirit.

∞

People that spark a person's wrath.

∞

People that fake a disappearance.

∞

People that take the **shady** path.

People that **use you** for "connections."

∞

People that befriend someone for "fame."

∞

People that believe they are "untouchable."

∞

People that are stubborn, and never change.

∞

People that are spoiled and rich and rotten.

People that think that life is "fair."

∞

People that don't get what they've gotten.

∞

People that pull your underwear.

MYSTERIOUS & COVERT

People that snap a person's bra strap.

∞

People that lick another's cone.

People that cannot get their facts straight.

∞

People that won't leave you alone.

∞

People that take a lot of effort.

∞

People that get under your skin.

∞

People that hatch a plot against you.

∞

People that try to **do you in**.

People that make a person hunger.

∞

People that make a person hide.

∞

People that bruise somebody's ego.

∞

People that hurt another's pride.

∞

People that have "ulterior motives."

People that call you **nasty names**.

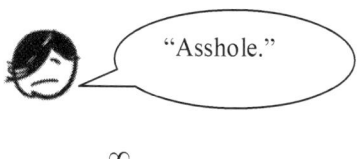

∞

People that give you sketchy details.

∞

People that seem to be **insane**.

People that **fuck with** your relations.

∞

People that bluster, brag and boast.

∞

People that "act like" they are psychic.*

People that don't believe in ghosts.

~

People that disregard the "science."

∞

People that keep you on your toes.

∞

People that block stem cells from forming.

∞

People that balk at UFOs.

*Except **real** psychics.

*Stephen Fry

MODEL CITIZENS

MODEL CITIZENS?

People that cannot keep their mouths shut.

∞

People that do not "walk the walk."

∞

People that put on too much jewelry.

∞

People that **talk** and **talk** and **talk**.

∞

People that don't think that you're funny.

∞

People that take the joke too far.

∞

People that think you're "much much" older.

∞

People that **forget** who you are.

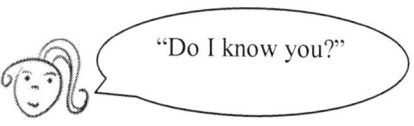

MODEL CITIZENS?

People that don't express their feelings.

People that can't make up their minds.

∞

People that serve someone a summons.

People that issue you a fine.

∞

People that slap you with a label.

"Bitch."

People that do not have good taste.

∞

People that **don't meet** expectations.

∞

People that "act nice" to your face.

"Hi."

"Hi."

1,001 PEOPLE THAT SUCK

∞

People that don't care WHAT you tell them.

∞

People that don't care what you SAY.

∞

People that turn their noses upward.

∞

People that just don't *walk away*.

∞

People that act like they're so "clever."

∞

People that single people out.*

As examples.

MODEL CITIZENS?

∞

People that judge you by your **color**.

∞

People that bribe you with their "clout."

∞

People that bait you with their "comments."

People that court you with their "wealth."

∞

People that **don't** care for their elders.

∞

People that jeopardize their health.

∞

People that stage an execution.

∞

People that seal a person's fate.

∞

People that don't pay restitution.

∞

People that don't appreciate.

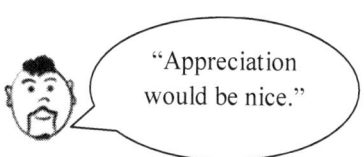

MODEL CITIZENS?

People that draw a **false** conclusion.

∞

People that like to hem and haw.

∞

People that try to beat the system.

People that don't follow the law.

People that **won't do** jury duty.

People that do not serve their time.

∞

People that do not set clear boundaries.

People that cross over the line.

∞

People that write you up a ticket.

∞

People that leave someone for dead.

∞

People that misinterpret feelings.

∞

People that claw to get ahead.

MODEL CITIZENS?

~

People that jump illegal borders.

∞

People that cannot take a hint.

∞

People that pimp out someone's daughter.

∞

People that don't offer a mint.

*Howard Stern

2

OUT & ABOUT

ROAD

"Did you ever think, it takes **8,460** bolts to assemble an automobile, and **one** nut to scatter it all over the road?"*

"True."

*Unknown

OUT & ABOUT: ROAD

People that do not use their blinkers.

∞

People that will not let you go.

∞

People that cut you off on purpose.

∞

People that drive too fuckin' slow.

People that ride on people's asses.

∞

People that **BEEP**, when lights turn green.

∞

People that stop, and pull you over.

∞

People that rubberneck the scene.

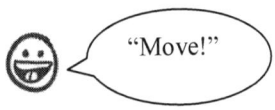

∞

People that tow another's vehicle.

∞

People that crash somebody's car.

∞

People that ride through on the shoulder.

∞

People that take ROAD RAGE too far.

∞

People that stick stuff on your windshield.

∞

People that splash you in the rain.

∞

People that **do not** check their mirrors.

∞

People that **hog** the left-hand lane.

1,001 PEOPLE THAT SUCK

∞

People that bump a person's bumper.

∞

People that run another down.

∞

People that stick you with their brake lights.

∞

People that follow you around.

∞

People that **do not** break for crosswalks.

∞

People that pepper you with words.

∞

People that stop short on the "on ramp."

∞

People that don't know how to MERGE.

BEACH

*Baba Ram Dass

OUT & ABOUT: BEACH

People that swipe a person's seashells.

∞

People that gawk, while at the beach.

∞

People that block another's sunlight.

∞

People that lay **beyond** your reach.

∞

People that push you in the water.

∞

People that spray you with their spit.

∞

People that soak you with a squirt gun.

1,001 PEOPLE THAT SUCK

∞

People that won't give you a sip.

OUT & ABOUT: BEACH

People that use up all the lotion.

∞

People that cut through people's wake.

People that hit you with their surfboard.

People that fail to take the bait.

∞

People that kick sand on your blanket.

∞

People that sit around and preen.

People that won't get off their high horse.

∞

People that don't say what they **mean**.

OUT & ABOUT: BEACH

People that steal a person's shovel.

People that give a person crabs.

∞

People that send out a "mixed" signal.

∞

People that don't know what they have.

People that don't have any substance.

People that make a lot of noise.

∞

People that smoke cigars on beaches.

∞

People that silence little boys.

GYM

OUT & ABOUT: GYM

People that **do not** put the weights back.

∞

People that don't wipe off machines.

∞

People that hog the bikes and treadmills.

∞

People that can't keep their nails clean.

∞

People that weigh in every hour.

∞

People that watch you on the scale.

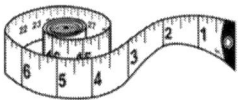

People that sap your motivation.

∞

People that **ROOT FOR** you to fail.

1,001 PEOPLE THAT SUCK

∞

People that beat you to the weight bench.

∞

People that won't let you "work in."

∞

People that click you with their cell phone.

∞

People that chatter, while you spin.

∞

People that snap you with a towel.

∞

People that make you want to cry.

∞

People that don't have any rhythm.

OUT & ABOUT: GYM

∞

People that *never even* try.

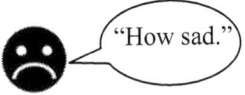

People that hijack the attention.

∞

People that flaunt their pecs and breasts.

∞

People that don't honor commitments.

∞

People that won't take **one more step**.

∞

People that break your concentration.

∞

People that **do not** catch the pass.

∞

People that interrupt the silence.

∞

People that **fart** in yoga class.

SHOPPING

OUT & ABOUT: SHOPPING

People that sell a faulty product.

∞

People that buy a stolen good.

∞

People that don't have any manners.

∞

People that don't do what they **should**.

∞

People that beat you to the checkout.

∞

People that try to cut in line.

∞

People that **do not** put the cart back.

∞

People that take their "sweet old time."

OUT & ABOUT: SHOPPING

∞

People that will not let you haggle.

∞

People that nickel you, and dime.

∞

People that **won't** refund your money.

∞

People that don't give you the time.

∞

People that put people "on notice."

∞

People that place others on "hold."

∞

People that call to telemarket.

∞

People that fail to break the mold.*

*Disappointing.

OUT & ABOUT: SHOPPING

∞

People that mess up someone's order.

∞

People that leave you at a loss.

∞

People that pay you with *all* pennies.

People that jack up shipping costs.

∞

People that do not give good discounts.

∞

People that never have a *sale*.

∞

People that place you on their "call list."

∞

People that send you too much mail.

People that call you "after hours."

People that put you on your guard.

∞

People that take the **ONLY** item.

∞

People that steal your credit card.

∞

People that ring you up real slowly.

∞

People that whistle catchy tunes.

OUT & ABOUT: SHOPPING

∞

People that do not want to help you.

∞

People that **hog** the dressing room.

People that crowd you in the aisle.

People that rush you at the racks.

People that **do not** stock your item.

∞

People that **do not** show some tact.

People that switch price tags on clothing.

∞

People that tend to overcharge.

∞

People that get "five-finger" discounts.

∞

People that don't sell X-LARGE.

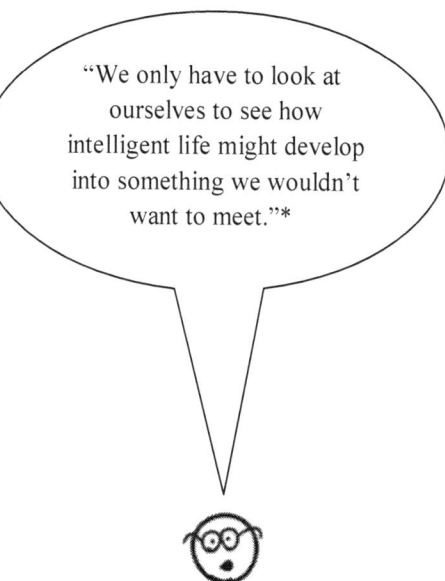

*Stephen Hawking

COLLEGE

OUT & ABOUT: COLLEGE

People that shave off people's eyebrows.

∞

People that serve too many shots.

∞

People that haze you, 'til you're bleeding.

∞

People that smoke up all your pot.

∞

People that see you through "beer goggles."

∞

People that hook up with your crush.

∞

People that want to date **your wingman**.

∞

People that don't like you too much.

∞

People that throw up at the party.

People that sponge and mooch and leech.

∞

People that sleep with the instructor.

∞

People that **don't know** how to teach.

People that don't prepare for lessons.

∞

People that put you on the spot.

∞

People that act real "goody goody."

∞

People that seem to be a **snot**.

1,001 PEOPLE THAT SUCK

∞

People that dunk you in the dunk tank.

∞

People that ruin someone's high.

People that peep into the shower.

∞

People that catch you in a lie.

∞

People that do not want to *RUSH* you.

∞

People that don't give you a bid.

∞

People that don't ask for your number.

∞

People that **don't**, and wish they **did**.

∞

People that act all "fake" and "phony."

∞

People that think that they're "so hot."

∞

People that seem real mean and prickly.

∞

People that tell you what you're **not**.

∞

People that kidnap someone's mascot.

∞

People that treat you like "the maid."

∞

People that make you feel real lonely.

∞

People that block your getting LAID.

*Lou Holtz

3

IN THE NEIGHBORHOOD

IN THE NEIGHBORHOOD

People that ignore their next-door neighbors.

∞

People that throw their pens at nerds.

∞

People that **do not** speak the language.

∞

People that use those "high-brow" words.

People that push you in the corner.

People that place you "in between."

∞

People that "act like" there's "no problem."

∞

People that deny the things they've seen.

1,001 PEOPLE THAT SUCK

People that take others for granted.

∞

People that use someone for sex.

∞

People that keep up with the Joneses.

∞

People that want to date your ex.*

∞

People that measure life in dollars $.

∞

People that don't make any sense.

∞

People that yell and scream and holler.

∞

People that do not pay the rent.

And do.

∞

People that talk loud at the movies.

∞

People that say you're not their "type."

∞

People that give a person *cooties*.

∞

People that buy into the HYPE.

∞

People that snub you at a function.

∞

People that rub you the wrong way.

∞

People that **do not** do their jobs right.

∞

People that don't watch what they say.

1,001 PEOPLE THAT SUCK

∞

People that make a person angry.

∞

People that put another down.

∞

People that run you 'round in circles.

People that drive people from town.

∞

People that **burden** you with problems.

∞

People that nag you with demands.

∞

People that smash your garden statue.

∞

People that take your garbage can.

∞

People that flaunt their wares on **Facebook**.

∞

People that "like" what others "hate."

∞

People that post a boring status.

∞

People that try to imitate.

~

People that **snoop** on people's pages.

∞

People that "hate on" other's posts.

1,001 PEOPLE THAT SUCK

∞

People that garnish someone's wages.

∞

People that burn your breakfast toast.*

 *Thanks.*

DOMESTICALLY SPEAKING

DOMESTICALLY SPEAKING

People that do not blow their noses.

People that breathe right on your food.

∞

People that **do not** put the seat down.

∞

People that catch you in the nude.

∞

People that love a person's money.

∞

People that like "first" children best.

∞

People that **do not** thank the hostess.

∞

People that don't attend to guests.

People that soon wear out their welcome.

∞

People that cannot *just sit still*.

∞

People that don't meet obligations.

∞

People that **cut you** from their will.*

∞

People that stomp on people's feelings.

∞

People that step on someone's toes.

∞

People that laugh at people's troubles.

∞

People that broadcast other's woes.

 *Whatever.*

∞

People that give someone an ulcer.

People that make a person sick.

∞

People that have a lot of "issues."

People that act like a real **dick**.

~

People that whisper things about you.

∞

People that talk behind your back.

∞

People that are **Good Christian Bitches**.

∞

People that show their "plumber's crack."

IN
SOCIAL SITUATIONS

IN SOCIAL SITUATIONS

People that **stiff you** with the bar tab.

∞

People that leave you in the lurch.

∞

People that wear "white" to a wedding.

∞

People that make you laugh in church.

∞

People that **do not** take their hats off.

People that **don't** remove their shoes.

∞

People that "handle" fruits at the grocer.

∞

People that give others bad news.

∞

People that turn the TV channel.

People that hijack the remote.

∞

People that delete your favorite program.

∞

People that don't get out, and vote.

IN SOCIAL SITUATIONS

∞

People that act like they are "perfect."

∞

People that won't hear others out.

∞

People that text, while they are driving.

∞

People that **convict**, when there is **doubt**.

IN SOCIAL SITUATIONS

People that **bug you** for your number.

People that hound you for a date.

∞

People that ask to sign a pre-nup.

∞

People that ditch their dinner date.

∞

People that run somebody ragged.

People that steer a person wrong.

∞

People that act "extremely" silly.

∞

People that *just can't sing* that song.

People that do not take a message.

∞

People that cannot take a joke.

People that laugh, when it's not funny.

∞

People that **do not** offer hope.

People that **write to** serial killers.

∞

People that censor books or plays.

∞

People that downplay global warming.

People that call for "**End of Days**."

HOLIDAYS
&
OCCASIONS

HOLIDAYS & OCCASIONS

(HALLOWEEN)

People that haunt a person's family.

People that egg a person's street.

People that poison someone's candy.

∞

People that don't give "trick or treats."

People that **flash** you on the sidewalk.

People that like to "ring and run."

∞

People that smash a neighbor's pumpkin.

∞

People that **don't** like to have fun.

(FUNERALS)

People that cut through death processions.

∞

People that blow off someone's wake.

(BIRTHDAYS)

People that skimp on people's presents.

∞

People that poke your birthday cake.

People that blow out people's candles.

∞

People that sneeze on other's meals.

(**OTHER**)

∞

People that put their kids in "pageants."

∞

People that make you spin your wheels.

∞

People that draw **unflattering portraits**.

∞

People that spin fictitious truths.

∞

People that **lurk** in people's bushes.

∞

People that corrupt the local youths.

(WEDDINGS)

People that leave you at the altar.

∞

People that step on people's veils.

∞

People that turn into **bridezillas**.

∞

People that ride on your coattails.*

Seriously.

(BREAK-UPS)

People that torch a person's clothing.

∞

People that hang you out to dry.

∞

People that take your **good** umbrella.

∞

People that leave you wondering

(IN ASPEN)

People that sweat a person's mansion.

∞

People that kill somebody's plants.

∞

People that spray you on the ski slope.

∞

People that start an AVALANCHE.

*Sophia Bush

4

PERSONALLY SPEAKING

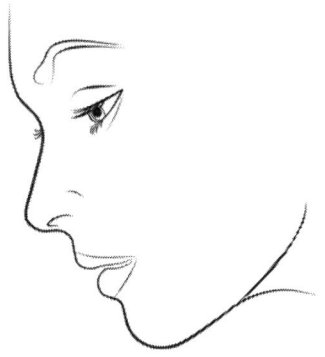

∞

People that aren't very friendly.

∞

People that don't care where you've been.

∞

People that **do not** act considerate.

∞

People that like to "rub it in."

∞

People that do things, just to test you.

∞

People that *always* play it safe.

∞

People that sit on the defensive.

∞

People that throw around their weight.

∞

People that peep through people's peepholes.

∞

People that "appear" at someone's door.

∞

People that object to other's weddings.

∞

People that act like complete **whores**.

∞

People that toy with people's feelings.

∞

People that play with someone's funds.

∞

People that palm a person's money.

PERSONALLY SPEAKING

∞

People that give their children guns.

1,001 PEOPLE THAT SUCK

∞

People that do not make it easy.

∞

People that tell you "**how**" to feel.

∞

People that say things that are "cheesy."

People that interrupt your meal.

People that make a bad impression.

∞

People that give you their cold/cough.

∞

People that try hard to possess you.

People that cannot *get you off*.

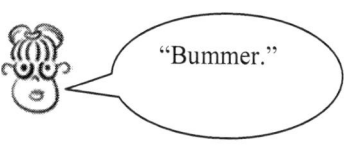

"Bummer."

PERSONALLY SPEAKING

∞

People that rate a person's sister.*

∞

People that force another's hand.

∞

People that overbook the airplane.

∞

People that take away your land.

 *Hot, or not?*

∞

People that "play like" they don't see you.

∞

People that elude a person's grasp.

∞

People that stand around and "posture."

∞

People that have **sticks** up their ass.

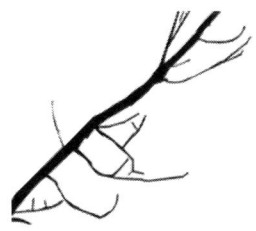

*Confucius (551 – 479 BC)

FOOD, HYGIENE & MANNERS

FOOD, HYGIENE & MANNERS

People that cause a lot of drama.

People that talk a lot of **smack**.

People that fail to keep it "civil."

∞

People that **do not** have your back.

People that **do not** wear deodorant.

People that don't take baths, and smell.

∞

People that use all the hot water.

∞

People that **do not** wish you well.

∞

People that trip you, when you're running.

∞

People that block your winning shot.

∞

People that try to be real "cunning."

∞

People that cake your clothes in snot.

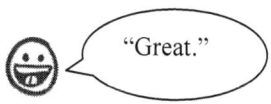

∞

People that urge you to have children.

∞

People that try to skirt the law.

∞

People that don't respect your culture.

∞

People that seem to "know it all."

1,001 PEOPLE THAT SUCK

∞

People that bore you with their stories.

∞

People that skeeve you with their feet.

∞

People that wake you, when you're sleeping.

∞

People that **do not** brush their teeth.

People that pick their nose in public.

∞

People that don't tell "funny" jokes.

∞

People that **never** let their hair down.

∞

People that drench your clothes in smoke.

FOOD, HYGIENE & MANNERS

∞

People that take a person's table.

People that spit in someone's food.

People that don't provide good service.

∞

People that give you "attitude."

∞

People that loosen pepper shakers.

∞

People that put up a "big stink."

∞

People that condescend to waiters.

∞

People that backwash in your drink.

∞

People that throw a "pity party."

∞

People that serve disgusting food.

∞

People that **will not** eat your cooking.

FOOD, HYGIENE & MANNERS

∞

People that aren't "in the mood."

∞

People that have a nasty habit.

∞

People that have some real bad breath.

∞

People that do not show forgiveness.

∞

People that **bully** kids to death.

*Tom Bodett

5

IN SCHOOL & AROUND THE WORLD

IN SCHOOL & AROUND THE WORLD

∞

People that pump up people's test scores.

∞

People that go and skew the curve.

People that slack off, after tenure.

∞

People that have a lot of **nerve**.

~

People that make false accusations.

∞

People that file outrageous claims.

∞

People that worship suicide bombers.

∞

People that don't see we're the **same**.

IN SCHOOL & AROUND THE WORLD

People that make a person fear them.

∞

People that squash a "just" revolt.

∞

People that patronize the public.

∞

People that recruit others for cults.

People that stone someone with pebbles.

People that violate human rights.

∞

People that mutilate young women.

∞

People that give up on your plight.

1,001 PEOPLE THAT SUCK

People that **aren't** altruistic.

∞

People that do things just for "show."

∞

People that kiss other people's asses.

∞

People that tell a person "no."

∞

People that curb a person's freedom.

People that kill your self-esteem.

∞

People that make the room turn "colder."

∞

People that **aren't** who they seem.

∞

People that **do not** pay attention.

∞

People that don't pay what you're worth.

∞

People that **don't** wish you "Good Morning."

∞

People that pollute the Planet Earth.

∞

People that don't make contributions.

∞

People that **never** volunteer.

∞

People that don't offer "solutions."

∞

People that **do not** want you near.

∞

People that wallow in their emotions.

∞

People that bask in people's pain.

∞

People that are always somehow "victims."

∞

People that "**can't recall**" your name.

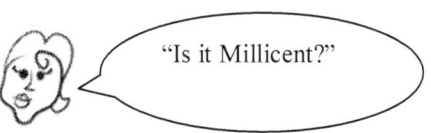
"Is it Millicent?"

∞

People that hack into your voicemail.

∞

People that interrupt your dreams.

∞

People that settle scores with violence.

∞

People that start up pyramid schemes.

*Wendelin Van Draanen, <u>Flipped</u>

6

DISAPPOINTMENTS

DISAPPOINTMENTS

People that **do not** want to see you.

People that don't come when you call.

∞

People that push kids on the playground.

∞

People that don't like you AT ALL.

∞

People that **do not** get to know you.

∞

People that go and pick you last.

∞

People that don't come to your party.

∞

People that will not sign your cast.

1,001 PEOPLE THAT SUCK

People that get in people's faces.

∞

People that stand in other's way.

∞

People that turn out to be **racist**.

∞

People that join the KKK.

∞

People that **do not** seek improvement.

People that do not try to thrive.

∞

People that park themselves on welfare.

∞

People that don't know how to drive.

DISAPPOINTMENTS

∞

People that pick at people's "sore spots."

∞

People that poison other's minds.

∞

People that do not grant your wishes.

∞

People that let you down in time.

1,001 PEOPLE THAT SUCK

∞

People that balk at your advances.

∞

People that act extremely **bold**.

∞

People that hate you, 'cause you're "pretty."

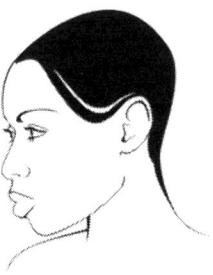

People that dis' you, 'cause you're "old."

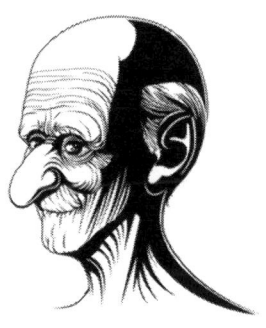

DISAPPOINTMENTS

∞

People that ruin reputations.

∞

People that make a person crack.

∞

∞

People that crumble under pressure.

∞

People that won't get off your back.

∞

People that do not treat you fairly.

∞

People that do not try their best.

∞

People that like to spread some rumors.

∞

People that act like a real "pest."

DISAPPOINTMENTS

∞

People that cloud another's vision.

∞

People that block somebody's view.

∞

People that do not keep their distance.

∞

People that go and lose their cool.

People that freeze a person's assets.

∞

People that take somebody's things.

∞

People that influence the jury.

∞

People that keep engagement rings.

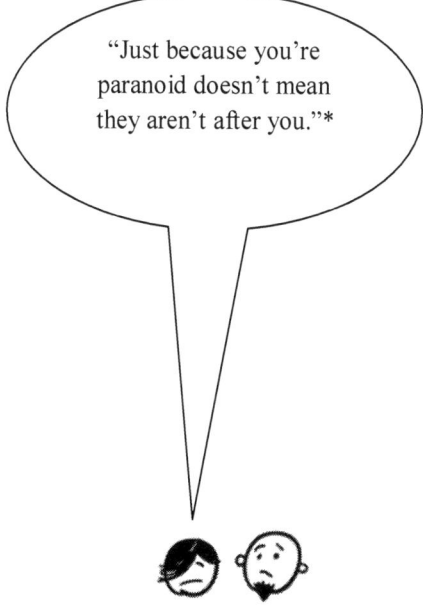

*Joseph Heller (1923-1999)

7

UNDER BRIDGES & IN CREVICES

∞

People that kick you in the nut sack.

∞

People that punch you in the nose.

∞

People that elbow someone's ribcage.

∞

People that snag your pantyhose.

∞

People that steal a person's thunder.

∞

People that take another's lead.

∞

People that prey on someone's goodness.

∞

People that **get,** what others **need**.

People that fight another's battle.

People that steal a person's friends.

∞

People that lack imagination.

People that overdo a trend.

∞

People that **do not** "Pledge Allegiance." *

∞

People that mock what you believe.

∞

People that have a petty grievance.

 *To the flag.

∞

People that make a person seethe.

UNDER BRIDGES & IN CREVICES

People that cramp a person's style.

∞

People that make somebody cringe.

People that are vicious, mean and vile.

∞

People that **will not** let you in.

∞

People that ignore your invitation.

∞

People that won't let down their wall.

∞

People that lose your reservation.

∞

People that eavesdrop on your call.

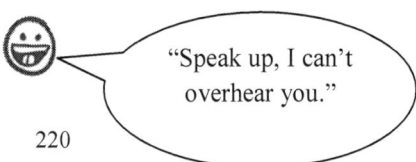

"Speak up, I can't overhear you."

∞

People that bump a person's shoulder, or that knock a person down.

∞

People that don't extend a handshake, or that fail to stand their ground.

∞

People that put you in the "hot seat."

∞

People that try and play both sides.

∞

People that have **annoying** voices.

∞

People that commit genocide.

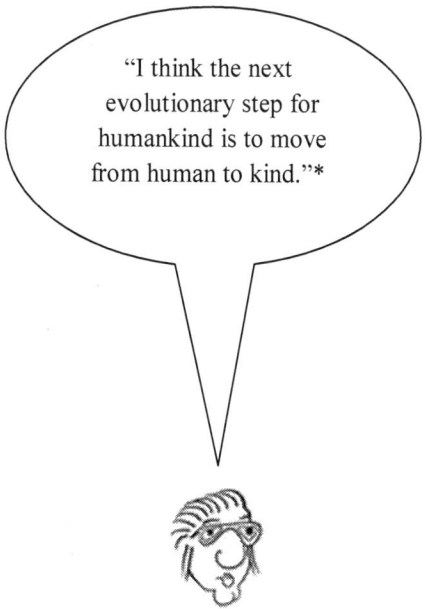

*Unknown

MEAN

MEAN

People that cause a person problems.

People that cause a person strain.

∞

People that swipe somebody's hubcap.

∞

People that steal your "baby name."

People that pick on people's siblings.

∞

People that pound on someone's door.

∞

People that act as instigators.

∞

People that start a "family war."

1,001 PEOPLE THAT SUCK

People that rob a person's grandma.

∞

People that rape another's friend.

∞

People that grade somebody's "sex act."

∞

People that return the gift you send.

∞

People that weigh on someone's conscience.

∞

People that stick in people's minds.

∞

People that walk through people's photos.

People that sneak up from behind.

MEAN

∞

People that trash a friend's apartment.

∞

People that tap a person's phone.

∞

People that taint a working crime scene.

∞

People that disrupt people's bones.

∞

People that **mix up** your prescription.

∞

People that mess with someone's meds.

∞

People that **can't** get it together.

1,001 PEOPLE THAT SUCK

∞

People that **fuck with** your street cred.

MEAN

∞

People that trump a person's triumph.

∞

People that spoil someone's fun.

∞

People that butt in conversations.

∞

People that think they're #1.

∞

People that give you the wrong number.

∞

People that make an idle threat.

∞

People that don't have good intentions.

∞

People that **haven't** earned it yet.

∞

People that glorify gore and violence.

People that glamorize sex and drugs.

∞

People that **do not** finish rehab.

∞

People that give you their bed bugs.

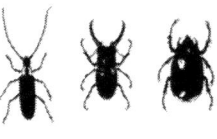

∞

People that don't remember birthdays.

People that point out people's flaws.

∞

People that call you up, to scare you.

MEAN

∞

People that give a person pause.

∞

People that give out ultimatums.

∞

People that feed on people's pain.

∞

People that block a person's efforts.

∞

People that **blacken** someone's name.

MEAN

∞

People that give you sloppy kisses.

∞

People that do not give good hugs.

∞

People that will not do the dishes.

∞

People that sell illegal drugs.

MEAN

~

People that put you on their "hit list."

∞

People that make you feel too tense.

∞

People that **ruin** your vacation.

∞

People that *shake* your confidence.

*Edith Sitwell (1887-1964)

VAIN & VICIOUS

∞

People that wear outrageous outfits.

∞

People that flash around their gold.

∞

People that put on too much makeup.

∞

People that don't do what they're **told**.

∞

People that push you in the limelight.

∞

People that pull you by the hair.

People that stomp you at a dance club.

∞

People that look at you, and **STARE**.

∞

People that are somehow always "negative."

∞

People that are often always "crude."

∞

People that can't make themselves happy.

∞

People that sulk around and brood.

∞

People that lash out at a stranger.

∞

People that gossip about friends.

∞

People that put others in danger.

∞

People that **do not** make amends.

1,001 PEOPLE THAT SUCK

∞

People that do not lift a finger.

∞

People that cannot chip a nail.

∞

People that put you in "positions."

∞

People that land others in jail.

∞

People that don't have any conscience.

∞

People that mess with people's heads.

∞

People that cut off someone's sentence.

∞

People that REALLY SUCK in bed.

*Miguel de Cervantes (1547-1616)

8

THE WORST

THE WORST

People that stick you with the phone bill.

∞

People that stump you with their clues.

∞

People that don't make time for children.

∞

People that **question** what you do.

∞

People that say "bad things" about you.

∞

People that give you crappy gifts.

∞

People that don't return your phone call.

∞

People that throw a *hissy fit*.

People that give away the ending.

∞

People that throw away their lives.

∞

People that act extremely jealous.

∞

People that tend to criticize.

∞

People that do not make it pleasant.

∞

People that **will not** make it work.

∞

People that don't live in the present.

THE WORST

∞

People that prove they are **just jerks**.

1,001 PEOPLE THAT SUCK

People that call a person "stupid."

∞

People that use you as a pawn.

∞

People that crash somebody's party.

∞

People that won't let you move on.

∞

People that dump on someone's mother.

∞

People that forget what others said.

∞

People that leave a person stranded.

∞

People that fake orgasms in bed.

THE WORST

∞

People that push you into marriage.

∞

People that trick you into scams.

∞

People that hunt endangered species.

∞

People that clog things up with spam.

∞

People that give you too much trouble.

∞

People that waste somebody's time.

∞

People that burst another's bubble.

∞

People that won't get off the line.

THE WORST

∞

People that fish for information.

∞

People that don't have any shame.

∞

People that **do not** make an effort.

∞

People that make you lose the game.

1,001 PEOPLE THAT SUCK

∞

People that peek at people's paystubs.

∞

People that bark at someone's dog.

∞

People that call the cops on neighbors.

∞

People that **stick firecrackers** in frogs.

*Elisabeth Kubler-Ross (1926-2004)

VINDICTIVE

VINDICTIVE

∞

People that don't return lost wallets.

∞

People that don't return lost keys.

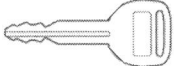

∞

People that sift through your belongings.

∞

People that bring you to your *knees*.

∞

People that do not stop to help you.

∞

People that put their feelings first.

∞

People that **do not** think of others.

∞

People that make it so much **worse**.

VINDICTIVE

People that curse in front of children.

∞

People that swear on people's lives.

∞

People that forget to pack the parachute.

∞

People that **ruin** the surprise.

∞

People that give you bad directions.

∞

People that string someone along.

∞

People that answer a question with a question.

∞

People that know what they do is **wrong**.

VINDICTIVE

People that bust a person's windshield.

People that key a person's car.

∞

People that slash somebody's tires.

∞

People that leer at you in bars.

∞

People that nose into your business.

∞

People that screw with people's lives.

∞

People that give you **no alternative**.

∞

People that "cheer," when others "die."

People that steal a person's taxi.

∞

People that stain a person's clothes.

∞

People that wear another's outfit.

∞

People that strike a person's pose.

VINDICTIVE

~

People that stand you up for dinner.

∞

People that won't give you a ride.

∞

People that cast you as a "sinner."

∞

People that **aid** a suicide.

VILE

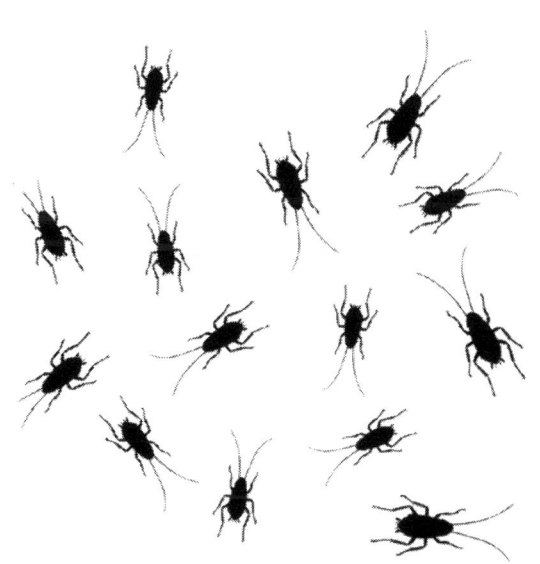

VILE

∞

People that pick through people's garbage.

∞

People that step in someone's space.

∞

People that "appear" in people's nightmares.

∞

People that **pass you** in a race.

∞

People that bust a person's kneecap.

People that twist a person's arm.

∞

People that desecrate your portrait.

∞

People that sound a false alarm.

∞

People that push you in the subway.

∞

People that will not meet your eye.

∞

People that tell it to the tabloids.

∞

People that **make you** tell a lie.

∞

People that cause humiliation.

∞

People that trick you into bed.

∞

People that question your credentials.

∞

People that **wish** others were dead.

VILE

∞

People that treat you like you're garbage.

∞

People that work you like a slave.

∞

People that sit on someone's headstone.

∞

People that loot a person's grave.

∞

People that dig into your background.

∞

People that are too tightly wound.

∞

People that do not have compassion.

∞

People that **build on** hallowed ground.

*John E. Pogue, <u>Everwood</u>

9

HEARTBREAKERS

HEARTBREAKERS

∞

People that don't know how to smile.

∞

People that don't know how to **share**.

∞

People that don't enjoy the *moments*.

∞

People that wish you **weren't** there.

∞

People that say "false things" about you.

∞

People that fill your heart with hate.

∞

People that issue you a death threat.

∞

People that make somebody late.

1,001 PEOPLE THAT SUCK

∞

People that hurt a person's feelings.

∞

People that break another's heart.

∞

People that leave you feeling "filthy."

∞

People that rip your world apart.

∞

People that put you in a pickle.

∞

People that place you in a bind.

∞

People that **will not** let you leave them.

∞

People that **do not** see the signs.

∞

People that stick you with a needle.

∞

People that stab you in the heart.

∞

People that **prick you** with their insults.

∞

People that pull people apart.

HEARTBREAKERS

∞

People that *aren't even* worth it.

∞

People that give someone "the hand."

∞

People that **back** a child molester.

∞

People that emasculate a man.

MORE PEOPLE…

MORE PEOPLE...

∞

People that **don't** report the missing.

∞

People that don't respect the dead.

∞

People that **fail** to honor veterans.

∞

People that **do not** call ahead.

∞

People that waste a person's money.

People that break somebody's things.

∞

People that threaten someone's purpose.

People that clip another's wings.

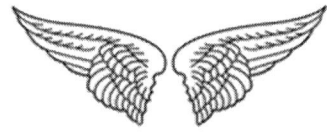

MORE PEOPLE...

∞

People that make a person crazy.

∞

People that turn somebody gray.

∞

People that give a person wrinkles.

∞

People that don't have much to say.

MORE PEOPLE…

∞

People that hold something **against** you.

∞

People that break a person's trust.

∞

People that try to circumvent you.

∞

People that **poach** an elephant tusk.

∞

People that try a person's patience.

∞

People that take somebody's pen.

∞

People that keep a person hanging.

∞

People that **leave you** in the end.

MORE PEOPLE...

∞

People that leave someone **forever**.

∞

People that **do not** say goodbye.

∞

People that don't protect your interests.

∞

People that make another cry.

∞

People that break a person's spirit.

∞

People that do a person **wrong**.

∞

People that make somebody tired.

∞

People that *just can't get along*.

MORE PEOPLE...

∞

People that catch you in flagrante.

∞

People that take somebody's turn.

∞

People that **aren't** kind or gracious.

∞

People that live, but never learn.

~

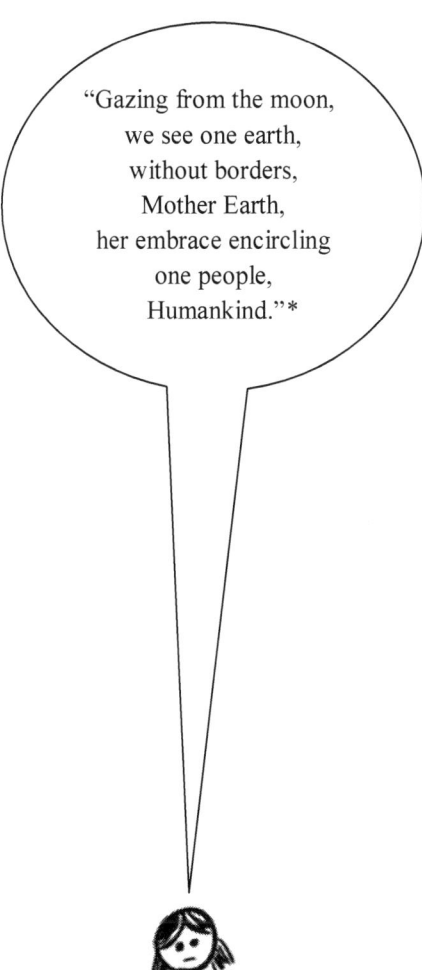

*Frederick Glaysher

To continue the discussion, please visit:

www.1001peoplethatsuck.com

ILLUSTRATIONS

Front cover, Beboy/Fotolia
p. 5, Fazakas Mihaly/Shutterstock
p.9, ARENA Creative/Shutterstock
p.10, John T Takai/Shutterstock
p.12, america365/Shutterstock
p.14, Glam/Shutterstock, Mastepanov Pavel/Shutterstock
p.15, John T Takai/Shutterstock, losw/Shutterstock
p.16, Banana Republic images/Shutterstock
p.17, stiven/Shutterstock, ARENA Creative/Shutterstock
p.18, Kalenik Hannah/Shutterstock
p.20, Cobalt Moon Design/Bigstock
p.21, Banana Republic images/Shutterstock
p.22, ARENA Creative/Shutterstock
p.25, Rorius/Bigstock
p.26, Kalenik Hanna/Shutterstock
p.28, lenm/Bigstock, Janos Levente/Shutterstock
p.29, losw/Shutterstock
p.30, Toonstyle.com/Shutterstock, Leremy/Shutterstock
p.31, Cobalt Moon Design/Shutterstock
p.33, Banana Republic images, Dimec & Janos Levente/Shutterstock
p.34, Asya Istomina/Shutterstock
p.35, ARENA Creative/Shutterstock
p.36, Theo Mailings/Shutterstock
p.37, Actor/Shutterstock
p.39, Carla Castagno/Shutterstock, ARENA Creative/Shutterstock
p.40, Michael Brown/Fotolia, ARENA Creative/Shutterstock
p.41, Pitroviz/Bigstock, Atlaspix/Shutterstock
p.42, Ray2012/Bigstock, ARENA Creative/Shutterstock
p.45, Banana Republic images/Shutterstock
p.47, shutterart/Bigstock
p.48, Artex67, Neo Edmund & Janos Levente/Shutterstock
p.49, HitToon.Com/Shutterstock
p.50, Skryl Sergey/Shutterstock
p.51, Cobalt Moon Design/Shutterstock

p.52, Jenny Solomon/Shutterstock
p.53, Janos Levente & Cindy Lee/Shutterstock, DeCe/Bigstock
p.55, Banana Republic images/Shutterstock
p.57, Andrija Markovic/Shutterstock
p.58, Romvo/Shutterstock
p.59, elfthryth/Shutterstock
p.61, ARENA Creative, Banana Republic, John T Takai/Shutterstock
p.63, Artex67/Shutterstock
p.64, Julia Lutgendorf/Shutterstock
p.66, Cattallina/Bigstock
p.67, lineartestpilot/Shutterstock
p.68, John T Takai/Shutterstock
p.69, Nuarevik/Shutterstock, Janos Levente/Shutterstock
p.71, Banana Republic images/Shutterstock
p.73, Carla Castagno/Shutterstock
p.75, Yulia Glam/Shutterstock
p.76, lineartestpilot/Shutterstock
p.77 & 78, Banana Republic images/Shutterstock
p.79, Janos Levente/Shutterstock
p.80, J. Levente, Toonstyle.com, Angela Sbandelli, DVARG/Shutterstock
p.81, Banana Republic images/Shutterstock
p.82, Mastepanov Pavel/Shutterstock, Janos Levente/Shutterstock
p.83, Matthew Cole/Shutterstock, Leremy/Shutterstock
p.84, zig8/Shutterstock
p.85, losw/Shutterstock
p.87, Banana Republic images/Shutterstock
p.91, Toonstyle, Banana Republic, JohnTakai & PhotoStocker/Shutterstock
p.92, Bekki Schwartz/Shutterstock, ARENA Creative/Shutterstock
p.93, Naturaldigital/Shutterstock
p.97, J. Levente, Toonstyle, Artex67 & Anna Tyukhmeneva/Shutterstock
p.98, Pagina/Bigstock
p.99, Kalenik Hanna/Shutterstock
p.100, Debra Hughes/Bigstock, Algol/Shutterstock
p.102, Matthew Cole & losw/Shutterstock, John T Takai/Bigstock
p.103, ARENA Creative/Shutterstock
p.105, Maluson/Shutterstock
p.106, inkspotts/Shutterstock

p.107, Rybkina2009/Shutterstock
p.108, John T Takai/Shutterstock
p.109, ARENA Creative/Shutterstock
p.111, Anna Tyukhmeneva/Shutterstock
p.112, Iveta Angelova/Shutterstock
p.113, Banana Republic images/Shutterstock
p.114, Sergey Furtaev/Bigstock
p.115, Janos Levente/Shutterstock
p.116, alexcoolok/Shutterstock
p.117, lineartestpilot/Shutterstock, Toonstyle.com/Shutterstock
p.118, tobkatrina/Bigstock
p.119, Banana Republic images/Shutterstock
p.121, Janos Levente/Shutterstock
p.123, Ice-Storm/Bigstock
p.124, lineartestpilot/Shutterstock
p.125, Andriy Zholudyev/Shutterstock, lineartestpilot/Shutterstock
p.127, Aleksey Zverev/Fotolia, Banana Republic images/Shutterstock
p.128, Georgios Kollidas/Shutterstock, Dawn Hudson/Shutterstock
p.129, ARENA Creative & Banana Republic images/Shutterstock
p.130, lkeskinen/Shutterstock
p.131, Darren Whittingham/Fotolia
p.133, Angela Sbandelli/Shutterstock
p.135, Potapov Alexander/Shutterstock
p.136, Janos Levente/Shutterstock, ocphoto/Shutterstock
p.137, Banana Republic images/Shutterstock
p.139, lineartestpilot/Shutterstock
p.140, Sergey Furtaev/Bigstock
p.141, lkeskinen, John T Takai & ARENA Creative/Shutterstock
p.143, Cindy Lee/Shutterstock
p.144, John T Takai/Shutterstock
p.145, ARENA Creative/Shutterstock
p.146, Martina Vaculikova/Shutterstock
p.149, John T Takai/Shutterstock
p.150, Janos Levente/Shutterstock, Banana Republic images/Shutterstock
p.151, Rybkina2009/Shutterstock, Atlaspix/Shutterstock
p.152, BasheeraDesigns/Bigstock
p.153, SoleilC/Bigstock

p.154, darrenwhi/Bigstock
p.155, Rybkina2009/Shutterstock, ARENA Creative/Shutterstock
p.157, gubh83/Shutterstock
p.158, fuxy24/Bigstock
p.159, Kalenik Hanna/Shutterstock
p.160, Dazdraperma/Bigstock, skvoor/Shutterstock,
p.161, Yana Godenko/Shutterstock
p.162, Slobodan Zivkovic/Bigstock, Janos Levente/Shutterstock
p.163, Christos Georghiou/Shutterstock, Banana Republic images/Shutterstock
p.164, Complot/Shutterstock, Banana Republic images/Shutterstock
p.165, DeCe/Bigstock, ARENA Creative/Shutterstock
p.167, Banana Republic images/Shutterstock
p.169, laura.st/Shutterstock
p.171, Art/Shutterstock
p.172, snap2Art/Bigstock
p.173, Leremy/Shutterstock, Banana Republic images/Shutterstock
p.174, outsiderzone/Bigstock, ARENA Creative/Shutterstock
p.175, Chloetru/Bigstock
p.177, Janos Levente/Shutterstock
p.179, Cienpies Design/Shutterstock
p.180, Barry Barnes/Shutterstock
p.181, Art/Shutterstock, ARENA Creative/Shutterstock
p.182, pittorebelyaewa/Bigstock
p.183, Janos Levente/Shutterstock
p.184, Anna Tyukhmeneva/Shutterstock
p.185, alexokokok/Shutterstock
p.186, Dawn Hudson/Shutterstock
p.187, Bibanesi/Fotolia
p.189, Banana Republic images, Toonstyle.com/Shutterstock
p.191, Kalenik Hanna/Shutterstock
p.192, lkeskinen/Shutterstock
p.194, ARENA Creative/Shutterstock
p.195, llaszlo/Shutterstock
p.196, anirav/Bigstock
p.197, Janos Levente/Shutterstock
p.198, Banana Republic images/Shutterstock
p.199, ARENA Creative/Shutterstock

p.201, Toonstyle.com & Banana Republic images/Shutterstock
p.203, Marisha/Shutterstock
p.204, Kalenik Hanna/Shutterstock
p.205, Bekki Schwartz/Shutterstock
p.206, candyman/Bigstock
p.207, Julia Lutgendorf/Shutterstock, CARBOUVAL/Bigstock
p.208, psynovec/Fotolia
p.209, ARENA Creative/Shutterstock
p.210, Complot/Shutterstock
p.211, Freud/Shutterstock
p.213, Janos Levente/Shutterstock
p.215, Ljupco Smokovski/Shutterstock, severe/Shutterstock
p.216, Alexkava/Bigstock, Forewer/Bigstock
p.217, Zorana Matijasevic/Shutterstock
p.218, lineartestpilot/Shutterstock, ARENA Creative/Shutterstock
p.220, ARENA Creative/Shutterstock
p.221, John T Takai/Shutterstock
p.222, ARENA Creative/Shutterstock
p.225, Banana Republic images/Shutterstock
p.227, stefa/Shutterstock
p.228, Banana Republic images/Shutterstock
p.229, Murika/Bigstock
p.230, Martina Vaculikova/Shutterstock
p.231, Janos Levente/Shutterstock
p.233, Mhlam/Bigstock, lineartestpilot/Shutterstock
p.235, John T Takai/Shutterstock
p.236, Zirka/Bigstock
p.237, Martina Vaculikova/Shutterstock
p.238, tokhiti/Bigstock
p.241, Banana Republic images/Shutterstock
p.243, Art/Shutterstock
p.244, Allaya/Bigstock
p.247, MartinaP/Shutterstock, milleriumarkay/Bigstock
p.249, ARENA Creative/Shutterstock
p.251, Banana Republic images/Shutterstock, Janos Levente/Shutterstock
p.253, Sashko/Shutterstock
p.254, Banana Republic images/Shutterstock

p.255, Nataly7/Bigstock
p.256 & 257, ARENA Creative/Shutterstock
p.258, losw/Shutterstock
p.259, WilleeCole/Shutterstock, Banana Republic images/Shutterstock
p.260, lineartestpilot/Shutterstock, vipervxw/Bigstock,
p.261, seamartini/Bigstock, Evellean/Shutterstock
p.263, Tkachenko Olga Nikolaevna/Shutterstock
p.265, CARBOUVAL/Bigstock
p.267, Digital Media Pro/Shutterstock
p.268, bigldesign/Bigstock
p.270, Cindy Lee/Shutterstock
p.272, Vaju Ariel/Shutterstock
p.273, SoleilC/Bigstock, Zirka/Bigstock
p.275, Vlada13/Shutterstock
p.277, svkv/Shutterstock
p.278, vorbiss/Bigstock
p.280, Squirrell/Shutterstock
p.281, Banana Republic images, Janos Levente/Shutterstock
p.282, PavelK/Shutterstock
p.283, John T Takai/Shutterstock
p.285, Banana Republic images, Toonstyle.com/Shutterstock
p.287, Dimanchik/Shutterstock
p.289, Mykhaylo Palinchak/Shutterstock
p.291, Miguel Angel Salinas Salinas/Shutterstock
p.292, Ultro_na_more/Shutterstock
p.293, speedfighter/Bigstock
p.297, ARENA Creative/Shutterstock
p.298, Donald Sawvel/Shutterstock
p.299, casejustin/Shutterstock
p.301, kathygold/Bigstock
p.302, losw/Shutterstock
p.303, ARENA Creative/Shutterstock
p.305, Volina/Shutterstock
p.307, Janos Levente/Shutterstock
p.311, Helga Pataki/Bigstock
Back Cover, ARENA Creative/Shutterstock

ACKNOWLEDGMENTS

I would like to thank my parents, Joseph and Carol Kochanski, for their love and support. I would also like to thank my sisters, Jennifer and Jill, for always being there. To my husband, Jim -- thank you for being you, and for letting me be me. And to my friends -- Nesli Damiani, Lori Smith, and Kerri Klein -- you are the most beautiful of butterflies.

ABOUT THE AUTHOR

Kerri Kochanski is an author, blogger and playwright. Her plays have been produced throughout the country, and in numerous New York City venues. Her work is published by Meriwether, Smith & Kraus, Dramatic Publishing, ICWP, and Applause Books. She lives in Greater Philadelphia, with her husband and children. For more information, please visit: www.kerrikochanski.com

Made in the USA
Lexington, KY
10 March 2017